Piano - Vocal - Guitar

Chart Hits OF '97-'98

W9-BQV-429

ISBN 0-7935-9386-7

HAL•LEONARD
CORPORATION
7777 W. BLUEMOUND RD. P.O. BOX 13819 MILWAUKEE, WI 53213

Visit Hal Leonard Online at
www.halleonard.com

Chart Hits OF '97-'98

CONTENTS

ALL BY MYSELF

Music by SERGEI RACHMANINOFF
Words and Additional Music by ERIC CARMEN

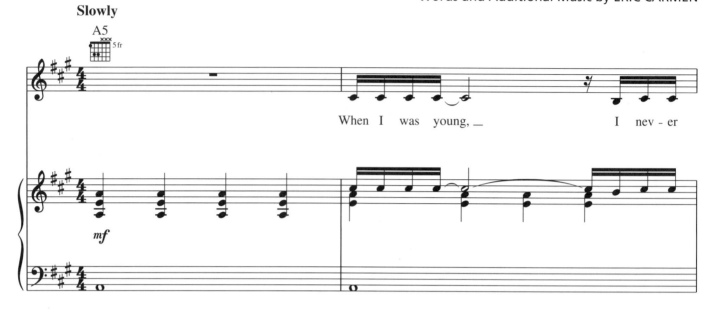

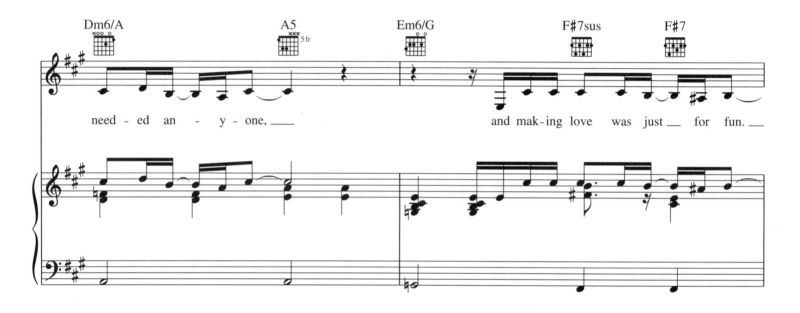

All Cried Out

Words and Music by BRIAN GEORGE, CURTIS BEDEAU,
GERARD CHARLES, LUCIEN GEORGE,
PAUL GEORGE and HUGH CLARKE

Original key: D-flat major. This edition has been transposed up one half-step to be more playable.

ALL FOR YOU

Words and Music by KEN BLOCK, JEFF BERES,
ANDREW COPELAND, RYAN NEWELL
and MARK TROJANOWSKI

(1., D.S.) Fin- 'lly I fig - ured out, but it took ___ a long, ___ long time. ___
(2.) I thought I'd seen it all 'cause it's been ___ a long, ___ long time. ___

Now ___ there's a turn - a - bout, ___ may-
Oh, ___ but then we'll trip and fall, won-

- be 'cause ___ I'm try - ing.}
- d'ring if ___ I'm blind. ___}

There's ___ been times ___

Fin - 'lly I fig -

hard   to   say ____ what   it   is _____ I   see ____ in   you. ____

BUILDING A MYSTERY

Words and Music by SARAH McLACHLAN
and PIERRE MARCHAND

BARELY BREATHING

Words and Music by
DUNCAN SHEIK

Well, I know what you're do-ing. I see it all too clear. I on-ly taste the sa-line when I kiss a-way your tears.

BUTTERFLY KISSES

Words and Music by RANDY THOMAS
and BOB CARLISLE

Smoothly

There's two things I know for sure. _____ She was
Sweet six - teen to - day, _____ she's
She'll change her name to - day. _____

sent here from heav - en and she's dad - dy's lit - tle girl. _____ As I
look - ing like her mom - ma a lit - tle more ev - 'ry day. _____
She'll make a prom - ise, and I'll give her _____ a - way.

drop to my knees _____ by her bed _____ at night, _____
One part wom - an, the oth - er part, girl. To
Stand - ing in the bride room just star - ing at her, she

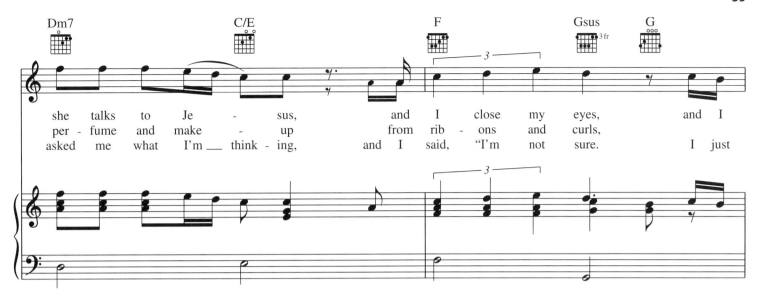

she talks to Je - sus, and I close my eyes, and I
per - fume and make - up from rib - ons and curls,
asked me what I'm __ think - ing, and I said, "I'm not sure. I just

thank God __ for all __ of the joy in my __ life.
try - ing __ her wings out in a great big world. _____
feel like __ I'm los - ing my ba - by girl." __

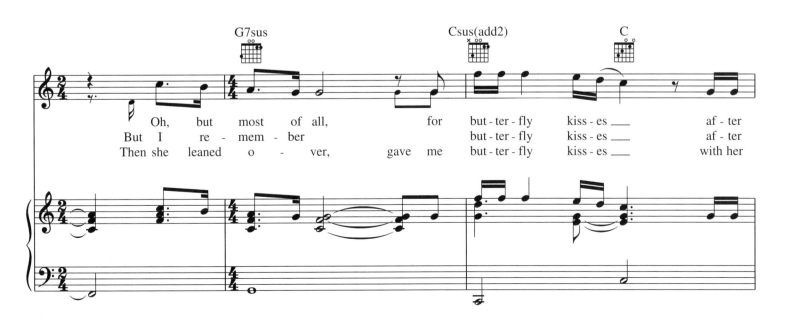

Oh, but most of all, for but - ter - fly kiss - es __ af - ter
But I re - mem - ber but - ter - fly kiss - es __ af - ter
Then she leaned o - ver, gave me but - ter - fly kiss - es __ with her

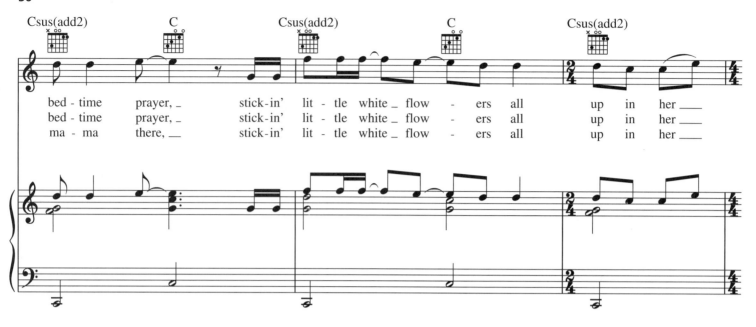

bed - time prayer, __ stick-in' lit - tle white __ flow - ers all up in her ___
bed - time prayer, __ stick-in' lit - tle white __ flow - ers all up in her ___
ma - ma there, __ stick-in' lit - tle white __ flow - ers all up in her ___

hair. "Walk be - side ___ the po - ny, dad - dy, it's
hair. "You know how much ___ I love ___ you, dad - dy, but if
hair. "Walk me down ___ the aisle, ___ dad - dy, it's

my first ride. ___ I know the cake __ looks fun - ny, dad - dy, but
you don't mind, ___ I'm on - ly goin' __ to kiss ___ you on ___ the
just a - bout time. Does my wed - ding gown __ look pret - ty, dad - dy? Dad-

ANDLE IN THE WIND 1997

Music by ELTON JOHN
Words by BERNIE TAUPIN

THE FRESHMEN

Words and Music by
BRIAN VANDER ARK

DON'T CRY FOR ME ARGENTINA
from EVITA

Words by TIM RICE
Music by ANDREW LLOYD WEBBER

Bright dance beat

vi - ta, E - vi - ta, E - vi - ta. _____

It won't be eas - y. You'll think it strange when I try to ex-plain how I

4 SEASONS OF LONELINESS

Words and Music by JAMES HARRIS III
and TERRY LEWIS

Original key: D-flat major. This edition has been transposed up one half-step to be more playable.

GO THE DISTANCE

from Walt Disney Pictures' HERCULES

Music by ALAN MENKEN
Lyrics by DAVID ZIPPEL

I have of-ten dreamed of a far-off place, where a
un-known road to em-brace my fate, where though that

he - ro's wel-come would be wait - ing for me, where the crowds _ will cheer _ when they
road may wan - der, it will lead ___ me to you. And a thou - sand years _ would be

66

I SAY A LITTLE PRAYER

featured in the Tri-Star Motion Picture MY BEST FRIEND'S WEDDING

Lyric by HAL DAVID
Music by BURT BACHARACH

(1.) The mo-ment I wake up,
(2.) I run __ for the bus, dear.
(D.S.) *Instrumental solo*

be-fore __ I put on my make-up, I
While rid-ing, I think of us, dear. I
(I

HARD TO SAY I'M SORRY

Words and Music by PETER CETERA
and DAVID FOSTER

Ev - 'ry - bod - y needs a lit - tle time a - way, ___
Could - n't stand to be kept a - way, ___

I heard her say, ___   from each oth - er.
not for a day, ___   from your bod - y.

HONEY

Words by MARIAH CAREY
Music by MARIAH CAREY, SEAN "PUFFY" COMBS, KAMAAL FAREED,
STEVEN A. JORDAN, STEPHEN HAGUE, BOBBY ROBINSON,
RONALD LARKINS, LARRY PRICE and MALCOLM McLAREN

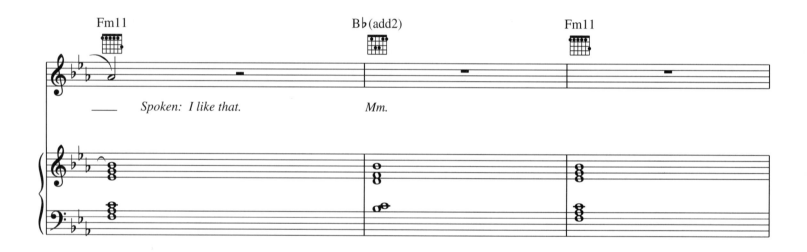

82

I BELIEVE IN YOU AND ME

from the Touchstone Motion Picture THE PREACHER'S WIFE

Words and Music by DAVID WOLFERT
and SANDY LINZER

I DO

Words and Music by
LISA LOEB

I DON'T WANT TO WAIT

Words and Music by
PAULA COLE

I'LL BE MISSING YOU

Written and Composed by
STING

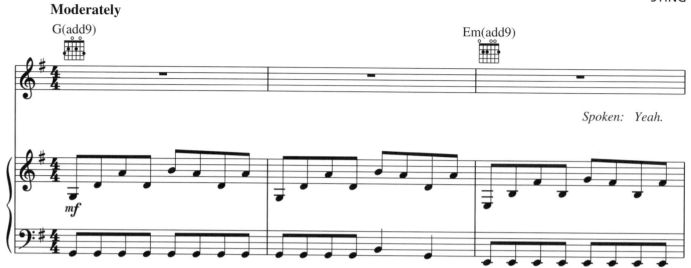

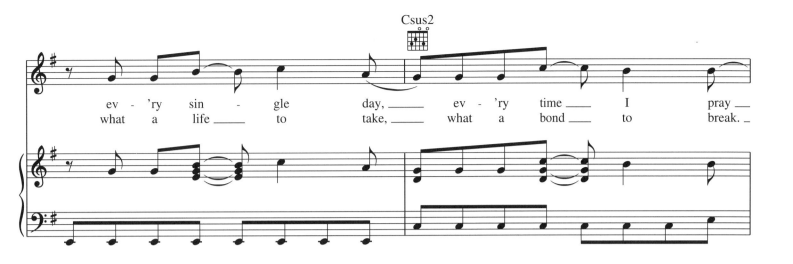

ev - 'ry sin - gle day, ___ ev - 'ry time ___ I pray ___
what a life ___ to take, ___ what a bond ___ to break. _

Repeat and Fade

___ I'll be miss - ing you. ___ Think-ing of the ___
___ I'll be miss - ing you. ___ Ev - 'ry step I ___

Rap Lyrics

Rap 1: *Seems like yesterday we used to rock the show.*
I laced the track, you locked the flow.
So far from hangin' on the block for dough.
Notorious, they got to know that life ain't always what it
Seemed to be. Words can't express what you mean to me.
Even though you're gone, we still a team.
Through your family, I'll fulfill your dreams.

Rap 2: *In the future, can't wait to see if you open up the gates for me.*
Reminisce sometime the night they took my friend.
Try to black it out, but it plays again.
When it's real, feelin's hard to conceal.
Can't imagine all the pain I feel.
Give anything to hear half your breath.
I know you're still livin' your life after death.

Rap 3: *It's kinda hard with you not around. Know you're in heaven smilin' down*
Watchin' us while we pray for you.
Ev'ry day we pray for you.
Till the day we meet again, in my heart is where I keep you, friend.
Memories give me the strength I need to proceed,
Strength I need to believe.

Rap 4: *My thoughts, Big, I just can't define.*
Wish I could turn back the hands of time,
Us and a six, shop for new clothes and kicks,
You and me take in flicks.
Make a hit, stages they receive you on.
Still can't believe you're gone.
Give anything to hear half your breath.
I know you're still livin' your life after death.

IT'S ALL COMING BACK TO ME NOW

Words and Music by
JIM STEINMAN

KISS THE RAIN

Words and Music by BILLIE MYERS,
DESMOND CHILD and ERIC BAZILIAN

MY HEART WILL GO ON
(Love Theme from "Titanic")

Music by JAMES HORNER
Lyric by WILL JENNINGS

Moderately

Ev - 'ry night in my dreams I see you, I feel you, that is how I know you go on.

NICE & SLOW

Words and Music by JERMAINE DUPRI, MANUEL SEAL,
USHER RAYMOND and BRIAN CASEY

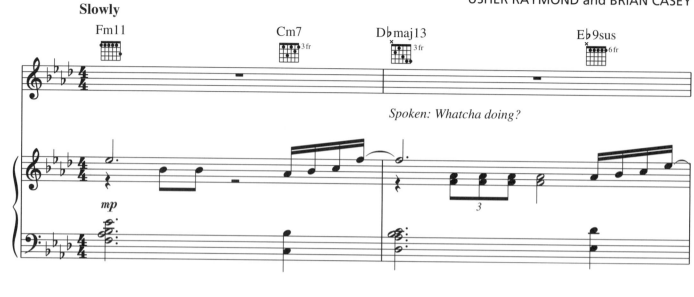

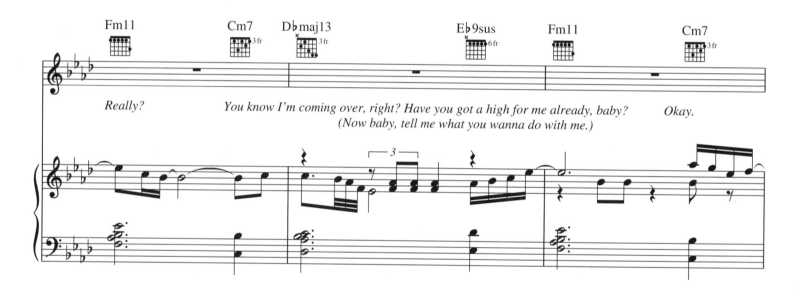

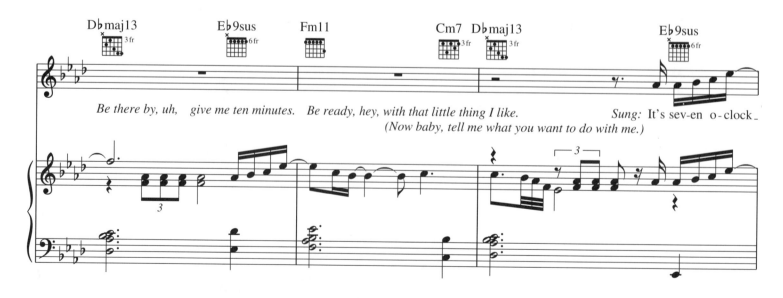

Rap Lyrics

They call me U-s-h-e-r R-a-y-m-o-n-d.
Now baby, tell me what you wanna do with me.
Gotta be in the light show to see
Every time that you roll with me, holding me,
Trying to keep control of me nice and slowly.
You know never letting go, never lessen up the flow.
This is how the hook go, come on.

SEMI-CHARMED LIFE

Words and Music by
STEPHAN JENKINS

YOU WERE MEANT FOR ME

Words and Music by JEWEL KILCHER
and STEVE POLTZ

SOMETHING ABOUT
THE WAY YOU LOOK TONIGHT

Words and Music by ELTON JOHN
and BERNIE TAUPIN

Original Key: F-sharp major. This edition has been transposed down one half-step to be more playable.

TELL HIM

Words and Music by WALTER AFANASIEFF,
DAVID FOSTER and LINDA THOMPSON

VALENTINE

Words and Music by JACK KUGELL
and JIM BRICKMAN

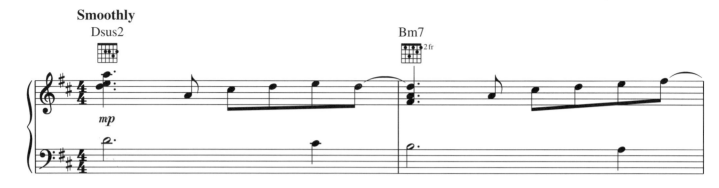

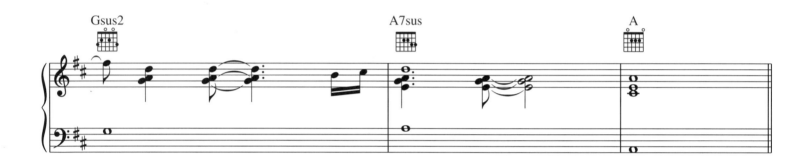

If there were no words, ___ no way to speak, ___ I ___
All of my life, ___ I have been wait - ing for ___ all

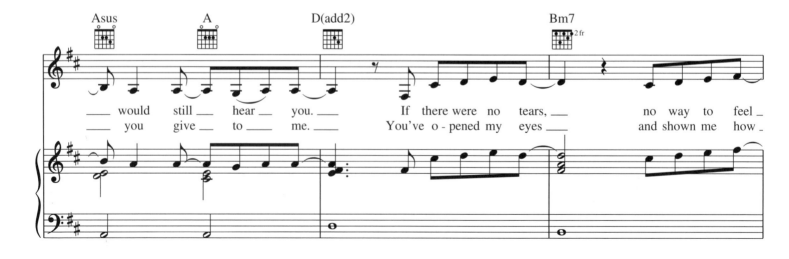

___ would still ___ hear ___ you. ___ If there were no tears, ___ no way to feel ___
___ you give ___ to ___ me. ___ You've o - pened my eyes ___ and shown me how

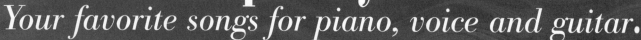